Forever a Member of the Pew!

Glenesha McIntosh

ISBN 979-8-9856703-3-2 (Paperback)
ISBN 979-8-9856703-4-9 (eBook)

Copyright © 2023 by Glenesha McIntosh

All rights reserved. No part of this publication may be reproduced, distributed, or transmitted in any form or by any means- including photocopying, recording, or other electronic or mechanical methods for commercial purposes-without prior written permission of the Author. The only exception is brief quotations in printed reviews.

Author can be contacted via:
www.gmsunshinedevotionals.com

Churches may reproduce portions of this book without the express written permission of the Author, provided the text does not exceed 500 words or 5 percent of the entire book, whichever is less, and that the text is not material quoted from another publisher. When reproducing text from this book, include the following credit line:
"Forever a Member of the Pew, written by Glenesha McIntosh, Used by permission."

Printed in the United States of America

Prologue

Dear Reader,

Forever a Member of the Pew is a book that's been silently brewing for years.

The Lord placed this on my heart as a confirmation of his expectation of us as children of God. Throughout our lives we will find moments, assignments, vocations, and lifestyles, where we are either in receipt of, performing, or walking in service.

No matter where we go, we will encounter many people in the world who are in positions that will cause us to either gravitate to, or retreat from them because of their approach, physical appearance, demeanor, manner of speaking, and disposition. We are indeed human, and the bible says that *"... man looks at the outward appearance..." 1 Samuel 16:7 NKJV*

But regardless of the way that we are seen or see others, we should not allow perceptions to dominate or disqualify us from the act of service. *"It was for this freedom that Christ set us free [completely liberating us]; ..." Galatians 5:1 AMP.*

"For you have been called to live in freedom, my brothers and sisters. But don't use your freedom to satisfy your sinful nature. Instead, use your freedom to serve one another in love." Galatians 5:13 AMP

We cannot escape service wherever we go, whether it be as customers, employees, family, or just our peers. But the Lord has placed special emphasis on the body of Christ, the Church. It is there that the Lord's body is re-membered, rejoined, reassembled, restored, and revitalized, every time we fellowship together. And each member has different functions. Year after year churches make room to re-structure, reposition, enhance, transition, and incorporate environments that welcome everyone. They nurture an atmosphere of service in love, and strive to facilitate the gifts, talents, and purpose of everyone.

Many stories throughout the bible can easily be viewed as miraculous and wonderful displays of healing, deliverance, and restoration. But if we take a closer look, they were all acts of service from the Lord himself, or his appointed ones, to his people.

The New Testament honed in on the lost sheep and one-on-one encounters where Jesus stepped aside from the multitudes, to cater to the needs of the one. Those *one's* in turn touched the lives of many with their extraordinary testimonies. And even today, he has not left a single one of us out of his will for us, as servers in the service of fellowship. The bible says that *"God has given each of you a gift from his great variety of spiritual gifts. Use them well to serve one another… Do it with all the strength and energy that God supplies. Then everything you do will bring glory to God through Jesus Christ." 1 Peter 4:10-11 NLT*

....

As we live a life of service within the various environments that we step into, let us not neglect to also be a part of service in the house of the Lord (**Forever being a Member of the Pew**); But rather, get plugged in and serve in the body of Christ.

*"Therefore, as we have opportunity, let us do good to all, **especially to those who are of the household of faith.**" Galatians 6:10 NKJV "... let us grow up in all things into Him [following His example] who is the Head--Christ. From Him the whole body [the church, in all its various parts], **joined and knitted firmly together by what every joint supplies, when each part is working properly**, causes the body to grow and mature, building itself up in [unselfish] love." Ephesians 4:15-16 AMP*

Be blessed,

PART 1

Stigma and stereotypes are often associated with many areas of our lives, and both rally around skewed and unfair beliefs, especially when it comes to groups and ideas that don't line up with the way others may feel, think, or act. Many of such stigmas or stereotypes are instilled as a child or shaped by the mainstream collective ideas that shifts, influences, and controls those who base their beliefs substantially on what is seen, announced, promoted, accepted, or publicized. And life within the church is certainly not exempt from the effects of such stigmas and stereotypes, because it contains the very same people that exist in various walks of life, outside of its walls.

Despite the nature of society, so many churches have nailed it, when it comes to the aspect of making people feel welcome. But to be moved to the point of participation takes much more than feeling welcome. One truly has to get past the many things that they were taught, the patterns of life, and the religious acts that sometimes differ greatly from church to church, sector to sector, and denomination to denomination. It truly is a culture shock from the moment you enter the church doors and meet new people from different walks of life. And as you learn and encounter experiences in the various aspects that you will come to recognize, it will ultimately influence your thoughts or considerations for engaging on a deeper level.

....

It is easy for those with talents and gifts to immediately feel a desire or envision themselves operating in certain functions if their spirit is moved, or if they feel inspired, and if the atmosphere lines up with who they are or where they need to be, to grow into who God is calling them to be. But for those who have not yet found their calling, desire, or interest, and may not have discovered what their talents and gifts are, it may be much harder to be motivated without the gentle nudging of others in love.

I grew up in church all my life, and being a part of the children's service was a given. If a child were to remain in the adult service, they were usually viewed as

Discovering the Beginning!

antisocial, overprotected, or just plain unseen by the other children. There were clicks and groups and friendships that took precedence whenever there were special events or services where the children were expected to participate. But in some strange way it motivated some of the others to try even harder to do their best at whatever it was that they signed up for, or whatever the leaders or their parents signed them up for.

There were many times I noticed the adults pushing the kids to do and function and be a part of whatever was taking place. At first it seemed as though they took a back seat and made everything about the children. They backed them up, supported them, sewed dance dresses, and made various costumes for the children to perform skits, sing, dance, recite, or play instruments. Looking back, the amount of time they dedicated to the children was nothing short of amazing. I'm sure many can relate to these memories.

There was a turning point though, where I think that the children motivated the adults to get up off the pew and discover what they still had brewing within them. I began seeing women's dance groups and pantomimes, duets, and small ensembles.

Then I started to hear the whispers of times past, when the adults were in their heyday, effortlessly operating in their gifts, before the children became front and center. What a beautiful earful of news to hear as a child.

But from a place where I was lacking a personal relationship with the Lord, all I could see was hard work and performances. I marveled at the dedication, frustration, stress, and the drive to excellence. The many hours put in, late nights, early mornings, missed meals, and over-worked routines; all for one day, one moment, or one weekend. I really couldn't see it from the side of the pew because I was right in the middle of all the happenings. Regardless of the many youth meetings and discussions about ministry and the importance of serving; many times I couldn't relate to the goodness of God because I had not yet had my own encounters with the Lord. So, although I saw responses brought about by the hearts of those who were moved by the Holy Spirit, I still was virtually spiritually blind to what that really meant for those who leaned in and those whose lives were truly changed because of what they saw, heard, and how it made them feel.

There are definitely children who hearts were captured by the Lord at a very young age. Whose encounters were surreal and marked their lives forever, as they experienced real relationship and connection with the Lord, displaying it through everything they did. I was not one of those kids. Were there moments when I felt swept away in the presence of the Lord, sure. But, those were moments that left imprints on my heart to be filled by the power of the Lord in later times to come.

I must say that in all of my years, participation in the house of the Lord became like second nature and helped shape me into who I am today.

In my early 20's my involvement matured into more than just participation; it transitioned into opportunities to serve. I had personally grasped that being a part of a ministry and being faithful to my assignment was an opportunity to be a part of the Glory of God.

> *Transitioning participation into service.*

It was a blessing to be a part of ushering in his presence and welcoming the Holy Spirit through many different forms of worship and reverence to him.

Of course, there were people who came to church, not necessarily to be changed and transformed, but because of tradition and religion, and to dress in their 'Sunday's best' and mingle with those whom they would only get to see on the weekend. But there were people who came to seek and to find something that they were lacking. People who came to lay down their heavy burdens; Those who came in search of healing, for prayers, for answers, and for community and accountability. It was in this place that I noticed that there were many who would walk through the door and walk back out either fulfilled or empty, but nevertheless, moving on a mission in their search of hope.

Don't let the excitement of youth cause you to forget your Creator. Honor him in your youth before you grow old and say, "Life is not pleasant anymore."

Ecclesiastes 12:1 NLT

Then [with a deep longing] you will seek Me and require Me [as a vital necessity] and [you will] find Me when you search for Me with all your heart.

Jeremiah 29:13 AMP

PART 2

Searching for hope is one of the hardest things to find in the world depending on what you're looking for. There is a difference between what the world considers as hope and the hope of the Lord. From a worldly perspective, hope is often used interchangeably with aspiration and viewed as a strong desire and expectation to succeed or accomplish. Many are often self-driven by aspiration.

The quest for hope.

Aspiration can also be viewed from a medical perspective, as the act of breathing in and out as well as the act of drawing out liquid from inside the body. But from a spiritual perspective, hope can only be found in the Lord. The Lord that is our desire and our expectation; He that has given us the breath of life and the blood that runs through our veins. So, the hope or aspiration of the world, is only made possible because of the Lord.

The bible says that God is a God of hope (Romans 15:13) and that he has plans to give us hope (Jeremiah 29:11). But even in his plans to give us hope, the bible doesn't only view hope as something that we acquire; but on a much deeper level, hope is viewed as something that we abound in on such an enormous scale that it creates a confident belief in the health, happiness and prosperity of what God has declared over our lives (the promises). This kind of hope is the gift of faith that constantly fills us with joy and peace and is fueled by the power of the Holy Spirit. A spirit that gives birth to fruits that will ensure that we are always walking in salvation, affirming the Lord's word that he will withhold no good thing from us.

> *Hope abounds in the environment based on the promise through faith.*

Psalm 23:1-3 NIV, says that *"The Lord is my shepherd, I lack nothing. He makes me lie down in green pastures, he leads me beside quiet waters, he refreshes my soul. He guides me along the right paths for his name's sake."* What a beautiful relationship that demonstrates the environment that hope abounds in. The Lord is promising us as our shepherd, that if we follow him, he makes sure that we find comfort and rest in the same place where he feeds us (his word). That he will lead us through life alongside the peaceful assurance of salvation that will constantly restore, reinvigorate, and quicken us from the deepest parts of our being. A relationship that allows us to live a life of abounding in the favor of goodness and mercy all the days of our lives that bring glory to God.

I think you can relate that there are times when we barely prioritize reading the bible, depending on the busyness of our lives.

I don't know about you, but I have acquired several books over the years; Ones that others have given to me and ones that I've purchased. They're all really good books; But in seasons where I have not even cracked open the word of God on my own, if I pick up any other book to read, there is a tremendous guilt that comes over me, because here is an opportunity for me to catch up and make up the time that I've so constantly missed in the word of God.

I say this because, there are so many times in life that we are just going through motion after motion, situation after situation and there never seems to be a dull moment, and when those silent moments actually happen, we don't always reach for the personal time with God.

Time for the word!

We may try to think of the best way to fill that time, that season, that weekend, with something from our list of things to do. We may try to plan some me-time, self-love time, rest and relaxation time, or a vacation. But we don't always think of spending that availability with quality time in the word.

Prioritizing time for not just reading but searching the Lord's word is purposeful and intentional.

We may pray or recite scripture somewhat frequently; but to actually sit and devote time to the Lord, is sometimes far or few in between our day-to-day course of living. We can pack so many activities into our itinerary, that the refreshing life that God meant to give us rest and comfort in relationship with him, becomes one of overload, hustling, seasonal happiness, exasperation, and strain.

There is so much to accomplish, so much to do, and we tend to balance the busyness of our weekly existence with just a couple hours of religious presence.

> *Busyness & the balance of routine pew-dom.*

It is here that many settle for the observance of routine pew-dom (the act of church bench-warming where one religiously shows up in a place of worship to reverence the Lord, but does not participate or exercise any service, talents, or gifts toward the function of the ministry for the edification of the Body of Christ) in the Kingdom of God.

For whatever was written in earlier times was written for our instruction, so that through endurance and the encouragement of the Scriptures we might have hope and overflow with confidence in His promises.

Romans 15:4 AMP

Be very careful, then, how you live—not as unwise but as wise, making the most of every opportunity, because the days are evil. Therefore do not be foolish, but understand what the Lord's will is.

Ephesians 5:15-17 NIV

PART 3

When I started reading the bible and actually going through books, not just chapters, I started to see how this Book of Life (the Bible), was interconnected with who I was in every facet of my life. I started finding out things about myself that I never knew; even feelings that arose within me for various reasons, allowed me to grasp the things and people that truly moved me.

For instance, when I read the book of Daniel, I truly admired the man that Daniel was. I was fascinated by the way that he spoke and what he stood for and most importantly, the type of relationship he had with the Lord.

> *Searching the Word and finding Relationship*

He was a dreamer, interpreter, and a visionary. There were things that were revealed and explained to him in his time, that the Lord trusted him to keep to himself. As a dreamer myself and the visual person that I am, I was truly intrigued by the detail and expression in all that God was showing him and how the Lord shared his secrets with him.

Even Gabriel, one of the angels confirmed the Lord's love for Daniel in two of his encounters with him. In Daniel 9:22-23 AMP Gabriel says *"O Daniel, I have now come to give you insight and wisdom and understanding. At the beginning of your supplications, the command [to give you an answer] was issued, and I have come to tell you, for you are highly regarded and greatly beloved."*

> The response of Love.

In Daniel chapter 10, verse 12 & 19 (AMP) when Gabriel appears to him again, he reconfirmed that same love and even touched him and strengthened him. *"Do not be afraid, Daniel, for from the first day that you set your heart on understanding this and on humbling yourself before your God, your words were heard, and I have come in response to your words."... "O man, highly regarded and greatly beloved, do not be afraid. Peace be to you; take courage and be strong."*

This same love that God displayed so attentively for Daniel is the same God that displays his love for us and has responded to us from the very first day that we set our hearts on his understanding and humbled ourselves before him.

Through his insight, wisdom and understanding he equipped Daniel with a heart to serve those whom he was called to edify, while faithfully serving the Lord. And he wants the same for us; A heart of service.

....

Do you remember the first time that you met the Lord on a personal level. When, you fell in love with everything about him. Just being in his presence made you want to stay there forever. You may not have understood everything there is to know about him, but you knew that he understood everything there was to know about you.

> *The first encounter.*

Your heart was for the Lord and his heart abounded in you. You walked with him and talked with him, and there was no distraction that took you away from experiencing his love. You were enthralled with all that he is and all that you saw and heard him do. His promises for you were nothing short of amazing, and the way that his Grace and

Mercy surrounded you faithfully, was unlike anything you could ever expect or imagine; and you saw his favor every step of the way.

But then, there were other books in your book of life, that meant you couldn't just stay in a place of being swept off your feet, but that you had to keep reading and experiencing the different books of your life that dramatically affected you in one way or another. This was the period where the flame in your heart may have noticeably simmered down and you began to realize that you have to practically apply this love that you received from the Lord, in and throughout your life, and it wasn't as easy as you thought.

Things become a bit more challenging, and the scale is always visibly weighing out the difference of what life is really like for you, versus the abundant life that God has for you.

... he himself gives everyone life and breath and everything else. From one man he made all the nations, that they should inhabit the whole earth; and he marked out their appointed times in history and the boundaries of their lands. God did this so that they would seek him and perhaps reach out for him and find him, though he is not far from any one of us. 'For in him we live and move and have our being.

Acts 17:25-28 NIV

I have told you all this so that you may have peace in me. Here on earth you will have many trials and sorrows. But take heart, because I have overcome the world."

John 16:33 NLT

PART 4

The bible contains so many books that draw similar reflections to different seasons in our lives.

Like in Exodus where you knew there was better for you, and you didn't have to constantly be subjected to forced bondage and suffering. But somehow in the journey of escape, there were moments where turning back to where you were before, the life you had, and the treatment that you were used to, seemed like a better alternative than the temporary wilderness survival situation you were facing in the moment.

> *A walk through the books of your life.*

In Judges, after finally getting to a place that felt like a long-awaited promised inheritance, to allow you to start over, you may have gotten comfortable and started to fall back in your faith, which caused the enemy to find opportunities to creep into your life subjecting you to various bouts of oppression. Your prayers then constantly became circled around requests for the Lord to raise up leaders and bring people into your life that you can depend on to make things right.

What about the book of Esther, where you felt like you had to hide who you were in moments when you needed to speak up, for fear of being persecuted. Or in Job where you just couldn't understand how you could have gone from riches to rags, from good health to pain and sickness; or in Ecclesiastes where you were just trying to discover the meaning of life, what is meaningless, and what is worth hoping for, living for, and laboring for.

What about Joel, where you lived through or heard stories about the invasion of your land, where many came in like locusts, eating, taking, and destroying everything in their path, without thought or concern for your well-being or your livelihood. When the land trembled, and the fire devoured, and the army of warriors did not skip a beat. When they swallowed up your inheritance and traded the boys and sold the girls; they carried off your finest treasures, and violently shed innocent blood. The grief that filled your heart after what was taken away from you, and the anger that followed right after.

In all those moments, do you remember when you first encountered the Lord? The one who loves you, the one who in the midst of it all, was trying to be seen and to be heard by you. It's easy for distance to creep in and widen into what seems like this major canyon, pulling apart your closeness with the Lord, especially, when you walked into the unchartered territories of the other books of your life. Did you remember then, what made you fall in love with the Lord in the first place? What drew you to him.

It's easy to forget about the promises of the Lord when all around you seems like loss and pain, chaos and struggle. Worse yet, is when we allow our relationship with God to move from such warm closeness to one that is stoic and cold. *Unapologetic storms & the issues of life.* This is the place where many can find themselves, after going through unapologetic storms.

At this point they can only view God as the high and mighty one, the one who sits high and looks low, the one out of reach, the one who just watched and did nothing.

Bitterness can creep in and fill the places where you had once reserved in love for him. This is the enemy's perfect opportunity, to begin to use your friends, and others around you to warn you that you can't have that kind of relationship with a God who controls it all, with a God who is beyond your reach. That you just need to reverence and fear him, do good, and never curse the one who still allows you to have an ounce of his breath.

It's real life. And sometimes, it's too real to talk about, to real to admit and to be emotionally vulnerable about. It's just too real to reveal. But you're not alone. Countless people have felt this way at one point or another.

It is here that many begin to struggle with integrating a life in Christ into their daily walk and lifestyle, prompting much change and the unavoidable experience of rejection, that causes one to rethink and reassess their established relationships and aspirations that guide their path in life. Some may begin to unintentionally, or intentionally compartmentalize their relationship with God, separately from their relationship with the world.

As I continued through life, there were seasons that took me further and further away from the passionate love that I had for the Lord; and in many cases I noticed that I started to need God's love in a more practical way. I entered phases where I needed him to show up as El Shaddai (God Almighty), El Elyon (The Most High God), Adonai (Master), the Ancient of Days (God), and the great I AM (Self-Existing God), more than as the lover of my soul.

But I must admit that those times indeed put my heart at a deficit. I was attending to my life, more than I was attending to the thing that God desired most, my heart. I needed El Roi (The God who sees me), Jehovah-Raah (The Lord My Shepherd), Jehovah Shammah (The Lord Who Is There), and Abba (my Father).

The God of my Life & the God of my Heart.

Me needing God on an intimate level, didn't take away from who he is in all his power and might; but I realized that I was missing out on his spirit. His spirit that allowed him to be my friend, my brother, and my father.

A love that filled the gaps in my life and allowed me to feel whole.

A love like what he had found within Daniel.

One day he got into a boat with his disciples, and he said to them, "Let us go across to the other side of the lake." So they set out, and as they sailed he fell asleep. And a windstorm came down on the lake, and they were filling with water and were in danger.

Luke 8:22-23 ESV

And they went and woke him, saying, "Master, Master, we are perishing!" And he awoke and rebuked the wind and the raging waves, and they ceased, and there was a calm. He said to them, "Where is your faith?" And they were afraid, and they marveled, saying to one another, "Who then is this, that he commands even winds and water, and they obey him?"

Luke 8:24-25 ESV

PART 5

We've witnessed those in the Bible, who have dared to 'call God out' by commanding, pleading, or even accusing. Each no doubt were met with God's consent, stipulation, or admonition, all leading towards his promises.

| *Bold moves!*

In the midst of war and conquering the battle, Joshua commanded God...

[Joshua said to the Lord in the presence of Israel: "Sun, stand still over Gibeon, and you, moon, over the Valley of Aijalon." So the sun stood still, and the moon stopped, till the nation avenged itself on its enemies,] Joshua 10:12-13 NIV

The bible says in Exodus 15:3 *that "The LORD is a man of war: the LORD is his name."* No wonder why the warrior in Joshua appealed to the man of war that the Lord is.

Joshua's conviction was embedded in his purpose as directed by the Lord with an interchangeable mindset of God's victory that was vital to the plan of God to possess his promises. Joshua considered not failure as an option, and exercised the authority of the Lord, as the Lord permitted.

...

In the midst of rebellious people, Moses pleaded with God,...

["Lord," he said,... Turn from your fierce anger; relent and do not bring disaster on your people.... Then the Lord relented and did not bring on his people the disaster he had threatened.] Exodus 32: 11-14 NIV

Moses considered not, that without the Shepherd constantly in the midst of the sheep, that the sheep would stray. Time and time again he moved God's hand of Mercy propelling acts of Grace under certain stipulations.

...

And what about Job?

Job considered not, that Satan had challenged God, not once but twice. The first time Satan drew reference to God, that it was easy for a man to serve God when he had a hedge of protection around him and all he had was blessed. So, Satan was allowed to kill, steal, and destroy everything that Job had, but Job did not curse God, he chose to worship.

The second time, Satan drew reference to God, that it was easy for a man to serve God (even after losing everything), but if his own life was threatened, to the point of affliction in his flesh and bones, that he will surely curse God. So, Satan was allowed to strike Job's body. Even his friends when they saw him was so troubled by his affliction that they tore their own robes and sprinkled dust on their heads and sat on the ground with him for seven days and seven nights without saying a word to him, because of how great Job's suffering was. And when Job finally opened his mouth, though he didn't curse God, he cursed the day of his birth.

...

It is nearly impossible for us who live and are born into a world of sin, to not experience similar feelings that come upon us almost instinctively. Having seemingly lost everything, and then being attacked in our bodies, mind, and our heart; Overwhelming

> *Instinctive Nature*

opinions that we are so close to death, can easily cause us to have negative thoughts, that we just don't want to travail anymore. And emotions of wishing that we were not born, can become very real; Even if it's only for a moment.

Job said *"If only my anguish could be weighed and all my misery be placed on the scales! It would surely outweigh the sand of the seas" Job 6:2-3 NIV*

When misery outweighs our praise, we are surely treading in deep waters. But God!

What do we do when the odds are stacked against us and we feel like our relationship with God has gone cold because life has overwhelmed us to the point where we are operating as if out of a cave, or on the backside of a desert?

> *When misery outweighs praise!*

… Where we've alienated ourselves from everyone, and are just going through our day to day with no real joy, happiness, excitement, or expectations. We're on a ship without a steering wheel, just going through the motions. We're not exactly lost; we're just operating without a purpose. Just a faithful member of the pew.

After going back and forth with his friends and determining that they were all *"miserable comforters"* (Job 16:1) with long-winded speeches, it became obvious that Job needed to turn his attention to God.

In the midst of his complaining he began to ask questions like, where would he find God and what would he say to him to state his case, and what would God answer and say to him (Job 23)?

> *Where is God?*

Have you questioned the possibilities of searching for God, what you would say to him and what would he say to you? If you stated your argument, would he oppose you? Would he press charges against you or find you innocent?

…

When you're in a place of being pressed on every side, the concept of Church looks a whole lot different to you. You may walk into church desperately needing something that the world can't give to you and searching for the presence of God. Some may feel that they just need a little Jesus, just to hold them over and keep them from feeling crushed; just until the storm passes. Some may realize that they need a lot more than good songs and a good word; they actually need a move of the Holy Spirit within their hearts, so that their worship can be for real, and so that their ears can be attuned to what the Lord is saying.

…

Nevertheless, there is a longing that tends to never leave us; When we can only but comfort ourselves with thoughts of good in times past, that offer a small light in the midst of darkness.

"How I long for the months gone by, for the days when God watched over me, when his lamp shone on my head and by his light I walked through darkness! Oh, for the days when I was in my prime, when God's intimate friendship blessed my house, when the Almighty was still with me and my children were around me, when my path was drenched with cream and the rock poured out for me streams of olive oil…" Job 29:1-6 NIV.

In the midst of a life deeply afflicted, Job began to search his life, not only for the good times and defining moments that he can rest his thoughts on, but in a desperation to appeal to God. He searched for every reason that would justify his innocence, and then he further accounted his unjustified suffering to the hand of God that has seemingly turned against him without cause. In moments like these we can find ourselves directly or indirectly accusing God for our situation.

The Search for Justification.

["Whoever heard me spoke well of me, and those who saw me commended me, because I rescued the poor who cried for help, and the fatherless who had none to assist them. The one who was dying blessed me; I made the widow's heart sing. I put on righteousness as my clothing; justice was my robe and my turban. I was eyes to the blind and feet to the lame. I was a father to the needy; I took up the case of the stranger. I broke the fangs of the wicked and snatched the victims from their teeth... Job 29:11-17 NIV

"But now they mock me... Terrors overwhelm me; my dignity is driven away as

by the wind, my safety vanishes like a cloud. "And now my life ebbs away; days of suffering grip me. Night pierces my bones; my gnawing pains never rest. In his great power God becomes like clothing to me; he binds me like the neck of my garment. He throws me into the mud, and I am reduced to dust and ashes. "I cry out to you, God, but you do not answer; I stand up, but you merely look at me. You turn on me ruthlessly; with the might of your hand you attack me. You snatch me up and drive me before the wind; you toss me about in the storm. I know you will bring me down to death, to the place appointed for all the living. Job 30:1, 15-23 NIV]

Job was truly in deep self-pity.

But a young man named Elihu who waited for his opportunity to speak. He brought the perspective that if we claim that we walked right before God and did nothing to deserve our current suffering, are we saying that we are right, and God is wrong? Elihu said that *"It is unthinkable that God would do wrong, that the Almighty would pervert justice." Job 34:12 NIV.*

No temptation [regardless of its source] has overtaken or enticed you that is not common to human experience [nor is any temptation unusual or beyond human resistance]; but God is faithful [to His word—He is compassionate and trustworthy], and He will not let you be tempted beyond your ability [to resist], but along with the temptation He [has in the past and is now and] will [always] provide the way out as well, so that you will be able to endure it [without yielding, and will overcome temptation with joy].

1 Corinthians 10:13 AMP

... for I assure you and most solemnly say to you, if you have [living] faith the size of a mustard seed, you will say to this mountain, 'Move from here to there,' and [if it is God's will] it will move; and nothing will be impossible for you.

Matthew 17:20 AMP

PART 6

In the New Testament Jesus said, *["Simon, Simon, Satan has asked to sift all of you as wheat. But I have prayed for you, Simon, that your faith may not fail. And when you have turned back, strengthen your brothers." But he replied, "Lord, I am ready to go with you to prison and to death." Jesus answered, "I tell you, Peter, before the rooster crows today, you will deny three times that you know me." Luke 22:31-34 NIV]*

This New Testament condition that we are still living in, was concealed in the Old Testament in Job. Satan constantly asks to sift us as wheat. But God desires that when that sifting happens that our faith does not fail. That we don't curse him, and that we don't go back and forth justifying ourselves and our righteousness, in comparing what we deserve and whether our good was of any value.

The truth is that in the day of trouble we too are not exempt from denial. We are not exempt from the feelings of being

> *The sifting that causes denial.*

separated from the Lord or from feeling like he has tossed us aside.

But do you remember Daniel?

The reality of Daniel's situation was that for most of his life beginning from a teenager, he was in captivity in Babylon. But that didn't take away from his purpose, gifts, and the way that God used him mightily for the entire 70 years of Judah's exile. He excelled and was chosen to serve in high places for King after King after King after King. But he loved God and praised him in spite of. Even after being thrown in the lions' den.

Joel chapter 2 has walked us through the very things we need to do when the period of Lamentation has come upon us, as a heavy brick upon our heads. Can you guess what is the first thing that the Lord says?

He says, Even now!

Even now, when your backs are against the wall. Even now, when you don't know how you are going to get by or through. Even now, when you feel like there is no up from here. Even now, when all you've heard is NO. Even now, when all you've seen is

| *Even Now!*

strife. Even now, when there is a series of loss all around you. Even now, when you are not motivated to get out of bed. Even now, when you find it hard to smile. Even now, when you are tormented, frustrated, boggled down, tired and worn…

["Even now," says the LORD, "Turn and come to Me with all your heart [in genuine repentance], With fasting and weeping and mourning [until every barrier is removed and the broken fellowship is restored]; Joel 2:12 AMP

[let the priests, the ministers of the LORD, weep and say, "Spare your people, O LORD, and make not your heritage a reproach, a byword among the nations. Why should they say among the peoples, 'Where is their God?'" Then the LORD became jealous for his land and had pity on his people. The LORD answered and said to his people, "Behold, I am sending to you grain, wine, and oil, and you will be satisfied; and I will no more make you a reproach among the nations…] Joel 2:17-19 ESV

…

God desires, Even Now, that we appropriate our suffering to the sifting and not try to blame him or find reasons to justify ourselves.

Because of Christ, the bible says that through reconciliation, God is committed to not counting our sin against us. *"God made him who had no sin to be sin for us, so that in him we might become the righteousness of God." 2 Corinthians 5:21 NIV.*

> *The righteousness of God.*

If Christ lives in us then despite our plight in life, we are already justified as the righteousness of God. Satan can use many different methods to continue to test our devotion to God, but if we only sit through it faithfully, week after week, we will forever be a member of the pew.

The bible says, *"Do not be anxious about anything, but in every situation, by prayer and petition, with thanksgiving, present your requests to God." Philippians 4:6 NIV*

Even if you have to turn down your plate and go to him in fasting, weeping and mourning. Push past the barrier of your pain and restore the broken fellowship. Get off the pew! The Lord is jealous after you and he will restore you. He will not leave you where you are so that people would criticize and reproach you and bring shame to your name and doubt the God you serve. He wants to see your heart after him again.

> Get off the pew!

Though God wants us to be present, the pew can cripple us into thinking that as long as we're present that God is satisfied. But the pew isn't service.

The bible says, *"God has given each of you a gift from his great variety of spiritual gifts. Use them well to serve one another. Do you have the gift of speaking? Then speak as though God himself were speaking through you. Do you have the gift of helping others? Do it with all the strength and energy that God supplies. Then everything you do will bring glory to God through Jesus Christ... Peter 4:10:11 NLT "even the Son of Man came not to be served but to serve others and to give his life as a ransom for many" Matthew 20:28 NLT.*

Jesus himself has set that example and as followers of Christ and sheep of the Shepherd, we are tasked with continuing the mission that he set out to do. Luke 19:10 says that Christ came to seek and to save. He saved through serving by sacrificing himself for the salvation of others.

... dear friends, we are convinced of better things in your case—the things that have to do with salvation. God is not unjust; he will not forget your work and the love you have shown him as you have helped his people and continue to help them.

Hebrews 6:9-10 NIV

Who is more important, the one who sits at the table or the one who serves? The one who sits at the table, of course. But not here! For I am among you as one who serves.

Luke 22:27 NLT

PART 7

I remember a time that I was looking for a church to attend and eventually serve in. I visited a church that had a large children's ministry with all the grade levels, and my children loved it. The word of God was being preached with love and conviction, but all of the elements just didn't come together for me. Why? Because the worship segment didn't move me. This may not sound like a big deal to some, but everyone's preference is different. Whether your personality yields thinker, dreamer, creative, artistic, worshiper, nurturer, greeter, speaker, etc., you find your groove in the atmosphere that nurtures who you are. The environment that challenges you, stretches you, looks like you, supports you and just as importantly, the environment that shepherds you.

Some like a soft-spoken Pastor, or a leader that teaches more than preaches. Some like a constant choir presence singing hymnals with organs and a traditional religious atmosphere, while others prefer smaller ensembles of worshipers, and even a more modern come as you are - freeing vibe. It looks different for everyone. But for me worship is a big part of the wonder within me that longs for the encounter that fulfills my soul in that way. So, I sat in the pew, and Sunday after Sunday, I began to feel like there was no place there for me. I began to feel like I would Forever be a Member of the Pew, sitting in the same row, same spot Sunday after Sunday, saying greetings to my neighboring members of the pews around me. It was comforting, but disturbing. I wasn't stretched, I wasn't on the edge of my seat, I wasn't moved to conviction, I wasn't moved to serve, and I wasn't even doing that spiritual rocking from side to side or back and forth, (some of you know what I mean 😊). That only meant one thing; Time to keep looking!

....

There are 2 "L" words that often get mixed up, and that is Loyalty and Love. I understand that people would stay loyal to the faithful pew and Sunday after Sunday dress to impress and be the best seat warmer around, but

> *Appropriating Loyalty & Love.*

that wasn't for me. A loyalty that brings love is earthly developed from the outside in, but a Love that develops loyalty is developed from the inside out, and that's what I was in search of. No guilty feeling or negative criticism was going to deter me from the places I knew that God had for me.

My desire was to serve, and to serve with a heart that bubbled over with a fullness where only God can say *"Do not come any closer," ... "Take off your sandals, for the place where you are standing is holy ground." Exodus 3:5 NIV*.

I'm sure that you've been places or are there right now, where in your walk, talk and maturity with God, you feel like you're right where you need to be. But that's presence; that's the pew, and it doesn't end there. Actually stepping out of your comfort zone and into your calling, your gifting, your service, is what draws you closer and closer to God and what he asks of you? Are you growing, are you stretching?

> *Presence to calling; Pew to service.*

Now, I know that service is not only confined within the walls of the church. There are so many areas of our lives that we can and do serve. Some of us live our lives daily in service just because of the career path we've chosen. And some of us perform random acts of service; just enough to boost our morale on a daily basis. But the reality is, that sometimes we neglect our service in the house of the Lord, because we consider our time spent there as part of our time or day of rest. So, we relax and enjoy the 'service'.

But the bible says, *"Let us think of ways to motivate one another to acts of love and good works. And let us not neglect our meeting together, as some people do, but encourage one another, especially now that the day of his return is drawing near." Hebrews 10:24-25 NLT.*

....

It all starts with love; Our first love. Not the one you first fell in love with, but the one who first fell in love with you.

"I knew you before I formed you in your mother's womb. Before you were born I set

you apart and appointed you as my prophet to the nations." Jeremiah 1:5 NLT.

The Lord is the one who had an encounter with you before you were even born, which sparked your very soul into existence. Even in the midst of turmoil, chaos and a world that constantly has changing views, thoughts, morals, and laws; Our soul continually longs after its first love.

> *Love births the soul and precedes delivery.*

"As the deer pants for the water brooks, So pants my soul for You, O God. My soul thirsts for God, for the living God." Psalm 42:1-2 NKJV.

Are you in need of an encounter that will restore the love that you had for the Lord? That Love that took away every ounce of shame, or regret, or fear. That love that had you constantly seeking to be in his presence eagerly seated at his feet,

> *Restoring Love is an Act of Service!*

serving at the table, smiling at the door, singing words of praises, ushering with joy, or dancing in his wonder. That Love that overwhelmed you, where you couldn't sit still. That love that made you want to get up off the pew and do something more; Something to show the Lord your devotion to him, acts of kindness, leaps of patience, mountains of self-control.

That Love that makes you not keep quiet when the question is asked, 'Does anyone need prayer?'. Love that allows you to open up to someone who offended you. Love that is open to connection and sharing. A Love that removes you from where you were bound and plants your feet where you are free without guilt or shame, but with excitement and expectation. A love that breaks the chains and enhances your life in notable ways. A Love that makes you feel like you are filled with riches even if your pockets are temporarily empty. A Love that always supports, always shepherds, always guides, always encircles, always draws you nearer. A Love that anoints and blesses. A Love that provides and favors. A love that makes you desire storing up treasures in heaven.

Are you ready to rekindle a Love that makes you not *"worry about everyday life— whether you have enough food and drink, or enough clothes to wear. Isn't life more than food, and your body more than clothing? Look at the birds. They don't plant or harvest or store food in barns, for your heavenly Father feeds them. And aren't you far more valuable to him than they are? Can all your worries add a single moment to your life?" Matthew 6:25-27 NLT*

[Then Jesus asked them, "When I sent you out to preach the Good News and you did not have money, a traveler's bag, or an extra pair of sandals, did you need anything?" "No," they replied.] Luke 22:35 NLT

People place such emphasis on earthly things, but you, in your beautiful need, can see every day how much he cares for you and how much he loves you and how, everything you need he provides. Not of your own doing but *God will supply. Do you trust him?* because of his favor and your dependency on him, he moves to supply your every need.

…

Jesus sent his disciples out to share good news and they didn't need anything that they depended on before. All he needed was their willingness to get up off the pews of their lives and serve, because the master had need of them to partake in the inheritance of the gospel of Christ. He promised to be a good Shepherd, so that they will always have all that they need. He promised that they will lie down in green pastures, so that they will have rest. He promised that they will be led beside peaceful streams, to that they can drink without fear.

He promised that their strength will be constantly renewed. He promised that he will always guide, always protect, and always lead them down the right paths, so they will always fulfill their purpose by bringing honor to his name as the righteousness of God. And they believed in his promises and walked in it.

Will you?

As you go through the books of your life, hold tight to your relationship with the Lord with all your heart, by ensuring that your intimacy with him, in his word (The Book of Life), is living (faith) **and active (works)**.

[Just then a hand touched me and lifted me, still trembling, to my hands and knees. And the man said to me, "Daniel, you are very precious to God, so listen carefully to what I

have to say to you. Stand up, for I have been sent to you." When he said this to me, I stood up, still trembling. Then he said, "Don't be afraid, Daniel. Since the first day you began to pray for understanding and to humble yourself before your God, your request has been heard in heaven. I have come in answer to your prayer.]

Daniel 10:10-12 NLT

His master said to him, 'Well done, good and faithful servant. You have been faithful and trustworthy over a little, I will put you in charge of many things; share in the joy of your master.

Matthew 25:21 AMP

A Message from the Author

Dear Reader,

If there is anything additional that I would leave you with, it's to never give up. Growth is understanding that because we only know a portion, then we are operating from a position of seeking wisdom to acquire the Lord's portion daily, which makes us whole.

Growth reminds me of the term evolution; a process of change in a certain direction, and that change brings development that happens over time. The Lord has apportioned to each of us talents and gifts, however we are tasked with ensuring proper investment. Investments require research, understanding, and a plan. Likewise, to find and grow those talents and gifts, knowing that we only have a piece of the puzzle, requires searching the Word of God for his portion, so that it can be connected to ours. That is what opens up our understanding and reveals to us guidance concerning his plan, purpose, and promises.

The Lord expects us to wisely handle what he has given us, ensuring that we do not hinder the process of change, in his certain direction, and in time we will see progress, maturity, and increase if we endure and do not give up.

God bless you.

G.M.

... continue to work out your salvation [that is, cultivate it, bring it to full effect, actively pursue spiritual maturity] with awe-inspired fear and trembling [using serious caution and critical self-evaluation to avoid anything that might offend God or discredit the name of Christ]. For it is [not your strength, but it is] God who is effectively at work in you, both to will and to work [that is, strengthening, energizing, and creating in you the longing and the ability to fulfill your purpose] for His good pleasure.

Philippians 2:12-13 AMP

Bibliography

Unless otherwise noted, all scripture is taken from the King James Version (KJV) of the Bible (Public Domain in the USA).

Scripture quotations & marked bible versions of KJV, NIV, ESV, NKJV, AMP, and NLT taken from:
- King James Bible. (Public Domain in the USA)
- Holy Bible, New International Version®, NIV® Copyright © 1973, 1978, 1984, 2011 by Biblica, Inc.® Used by permission. All rights reserved worldwide.
- The ESV® Bible (The Holy Bible, English Standard Version®) copyright © 2001 by Crossway Bibles, a publishing ministry of Good News Publishers.
- The Holy Bible, New King James Version, Copyright © 1982 Thomas Nelson. All rights reserved.
- Amplified Bible Copyright © 2015 by The Lockman Foundation. All rights reserved www.lockman.org

- Holy Bible, New Living Translation, copyright © 1996, 2004, 2015 by Tyndale House Foundation. Used by permission of Tyndale House Publishers, Inc., Carol Stream, Illinois 60188. All rights reserved.
- NIV & KJV Side-by-Side Bible Published by Zondervan www.zondervan.com

Word Search, Synonyms, and Definitions taken from:
- https://www.google.com/search?
- https://www.thesaurus.com/browse/ ©2019 Dictionary.com, LLC
- Merriam-Webster Online (www.Merriam-Webster.com)
- Merriam-Webster Online Dictionary copyright © 2015 by Merriam-Webster, Incorporated
- Merriam-Webster Online Thesaurus copyright © 2015 by Merriam-Webster, Incorporated

12 Biblical Facts about Daniel by Jeffrey Kranz | Oct 29, 2016 | Bible characters, Bible facts

- https://overviewbible.com/prophet-daniel-facts/

www.ingramcontent.com/pod-product-compliance
Lightning Source LLC
Chambersburg PA
CBHW060316050426
42449CB00028B/2086